FROM **Atheist** TO *Ambassador*

The First Sixty Years

James R Hall II

WESTBOW·
PRESS
A DIVISION OF THOMAS NELSON
& ZONDERVAN

WestBow Press books may be ordered through booksellers or by contacting:

WestBow Press
A Division of Thomas Nelson & Zondervan
1663 Liberty Drive
Bloomington, IN 47403
www.westbowpress.com
1 (866) 928-1240

ISBN: 978-1-4908-4090-1 (sc)
ISBN: 978-1-4908-4089-5 (hc)
ISBN: 978-1-4908-4091-8 (e)

Library of Congress Control Number: 2014910790

Printed in the United States of America.

WestBow Press rev. date: 6/30/2014

CONTENTS

PREFACE

Definitions by Dictionary.com

Atheist: A person who denies or disbelieves the existence of a supreme being or beings.

Ambassador: 1. a diplomatic official of the highest rank, sent by one sovereign or state to another as its resident representative. 2. an authorized messenger or representative.

I want to say first of all thank you for the opportunity for allowing me to share a portion of my life and testimony with you. My name is James R Hall II, and I want to give God all of the glory for any good that comes out of this piece of work. For it was God that has made it all possible and who has given me the inspiration to put this book together. It would take me a long time and a lot of ink and paper to tell you of all that God has done for me, and all of the things that would go along with it. There will be a lot that I will leave out that happened in my life on purpose some names of people and places.

I do want to say thank you to my pastors, Pastor Alfred Deeds, the late Pastor Lonnie Marcus, and my present pastor, Dr Ronald Eagleton. God put these men in my life to add certain things such as anointing, teaching, and dedication through observation and teaching. These men of God were and have been very patient with me and have made a difference in my life that will last an eternity. Again I want to say thank you for pastoring me over the last thirty-seven years as of this writing.

I've added to the title "The First Sixty Years" because on October 5, 2011, I turned sixty years of age. The Word of God says in Genesis 6:3 God has promised me 120 years, so I am halfway there, and should the LORD tarry, I want to be able to blow out my own candles on my 120th birthday.

CHAPTER 1

A RELIGIOUS MOM

Catherine Hall and I first met face to face on October 5, 1951, in South Bend, Indiana. I thank God for my mother—I've called her Mom all of my life—and I believe she was an exceptional woman.

She was married to one man, James R Hall Sr., who was the father of all her thirteen children—yes, I said thirteen children: ten girls and three boys. That included two sets of boy/girl twins. I would list their nicknames, but once they read this book, I'm confident they would pool their money together and put a hit out on me. The given names are Gail, Janice, Sandra, James (that's me), Beverly, Belinda, Phyllis, Michael and Michelle (first set of twins), Marilyn, Gwen and George (second set), and Sheila.

Now you can understand why I consider my mother exceptional. None of my siblings and I were ever dropped off at a day care, and we all started school at the age of five or earlier. My mother cooked every day—sometimes two or three times a day—along with washing and drying clothes on a clothesline outside and having them all ironed, folded, and put away before the day was over.

My mom kept a clean house and clean children. Obviously, she took time for her husband, which resulted in the thirteen of us. And as I look back, I can see that it was up to her to make the house (as small as it was) the home it was.

My dad was a good father, a hardworking man, and a good provider for the household. He showed me how to plant a garden, which helped provide food for the year. He worked two jobs at a time, if needed, to pay the bills and keep food on the table, even giving us an allowance every now and then when he thought we deserved it, even if it was just a quarter every two weeks. But it was our mom who tried to tell us to not to spend it all at once and save some for later in the week when the ice cream truck would come around and for Sunday school.

The only reason we went to Sunday school was because Mom was there most of the time watching us. Dad made sure we went every week, but I can't remember him ever going with us. He gave us change to put in Sunday school, but he almost never went, though he made sure we respected the pastors in the neighborhood.

In Sunday school, we were taught with those little flashcards that had a picture on one side and Scriptures and a story on the reverse side. There were no separate rooms to go to because the church house was just one big room. We would split up into different sections of the church and have our classes. There were only four classes: the men's class, the women's class, the young adult class, and the children's class.

If you're a Sunday school teacher, never take lightly the lessons that you teach to children. I say that because some of the seeds that were planted in me in Sunday school are still growing today in my life.

As I look back, I can remember only two times that Dad came to church: Mother's Day and an Easter service. Mom was the one whom we looked up to for a spiritual example and leader in our early childhood. I remember attempting to read and understand some things in the Bible as a child of about nine or ten years. I didn't go to my dad for help understanding but to my mom. She might not have known the answers, but she did encourage me to keep reading.

My mom was the one in our household who knew God. If someone in the house got sick, it was our mom who prayed. When the Bible was read, it was under Mom's guidance. I think the main reason my mom acted the way she did was because she had a religious mother who faithfully attended church, read her Bible, and prayed all the time. I never knew the depth of my mom's relationship with God—and that's only for God and her to know—but I do know that she prayed for and loved her children very much.

I noticed times that, when the pastor preached, tears slid down my mother's face, and her knee bobbed up and down as the heel of her shoe tapped the wooden floor. She and the rest of the women in the church would feel the Spirit of God as His Word went forth. It sounded like a train going by if you didn't know any better, which I didn't. As the pastor preached harder, the harder the women would tap their heels, and it sounded like a train coming, passing, and leaving as the message began to come to an end.

How can you measure a mother's love for her children? Simply by how she takes care of them, teaches them, and prepares them for when she won't be around. My mother taught me how to cook (I've been told that I'm pretty good at it), clean, wash, and iron my clothes. My mom always said in her later years, "I did the best I could." My siblings and I always responded, "And you did a good job." She gave us all that she knew and all that she knew about God, and I'm proud to say that today, all thirteen of her children have a relationship with God, and most are active in the church.

Thank you, Mom, for giving us some of what you had and trusting God to do the rest.

CHAPTER 2

A SICK SON

Sickle cell disease is one of most horrific conditions that can happen to a child of African American descent. There have been a few cases of the disease found in those of Hispanic and Asian descent, but it's predominantly a disease among African Americans. One in three African Americans will be affected by sickle cell, either with the disease or the trait.

Out of thirteen children, three of us had sickle cell disease: me; my sister Beverly, who was one year younger than me; and my baby sister Sheila. I won't tell their stories because one day they may want to write a book as well. As for me, I was the first of us to suffer with this disease. It has been known to not only make you physically sick but to kill some sufferers with the unbearable pain.

As a child, I was constantly sick from having what my family called a crisis. This was when my red blood cells would go from soft, pliable ovals that could carry oxygen to different parts of the body to sickle-shaped cells with hard shells that couldn't carry oxygen. Instead, they would collect in my joints, causing excruciating pain.

The main treatment back then was to give something to relieve the pain, a lot of oxygen, and a lot of rest. Blood transfusions to replace the blood that had gone bad were also a common practice for treating a crisis. After a week or two in the hospital, I was back to normal—for the time being.

It was hard being a kid and having sickle cell disease. I could play with the other kids in the neighborhood, but I couldn't play for as long as they did. Much as my family liked to swim, I rarely could go swimming without getting sick or coming down with a crisis. It was something about my body getting cold and tired that would make me sick or bring on a crisis. Sometimes I could avoid a trip to the hospital if I could get my body warmed up quickly and take something to ease the pain. My mother would use hot water bottles and even an iron on low setting with towels on the area that was cold to try to warm up my body. To this day, I don't like being cold.

During the first thirty years of my life, I had countless blood transfusions. My one employer had blood drives for me because I needed so many and insurance wouldn't cover all of the cost. The blood had to be cross-matched before I received a transfusion, and the more transfusions I had, the harder it was to find the right match. Every time I receive a transfusion, I pick up different characteristics of the blood I receive. So when I'm matched for the next transfusion, they have to match all the properties of my current blood. There are properties that I have picked up in the past that still affect me today.

My parents did the best they knew how to help me with my illness. My parents tried to tell me that, because of my illness, I had to look out for myself, regardless of what my friends were doing. I didn't always listen and suffered the consequences time and time again. Once I began to feel better after a crisis, I thought that I could run and play like my friends, stay out all night, and just treat my body any way I wanted—until I got sick again.

Sickle cell wears down your body by trying to compensate for a lack of oxygen, which keeps your body from developing at a normal rate. It also can damage internal organs such as the liver, kidneys, and spleen, and eventually the heart, which works so hard to pump more blood with less oxygen in it.

Then there were the pain medications: Vicodin, Darvon, morphine, Motrin, Tylenol 3, plus penicillin and other antibiotics for infections and many more medications that I can't remember now.

Let me say a word about doctors and medication. I appreciate all my doctors' efforts to make me feel better and get me back to a normal life. When it's said that doctors are practicing medicine, I can relate to that firsthand. I had a doctor prescribe some penicillin while I was in the hospital one time. I don't know if the dosage was too high or what, but the next day the top layer of my skin began to peel completely off! Within three to four days I had shed all of my skin and had a new layer of skin. It was not a painful ordeal, but it scared the heck out of the doctor because of what he prescribed as he practiced to see what would work for me best. When it came to relieving pain, it seemed my body responded best to Demerol, which is a brand of Meperidine, a narcotic compound used as an analgesic (pain reliever) and sedative. It not only knocked out the pain, but also knocked me out, and when it began to wear off, I felt as though I was lightly falling from space. From being in excruciating pain to feeling as though you are floating on a cloud, yes, you can get attached to wanting to feel like that as an alternative to pain. Thank God that I never got addicted to pain medicine, but I can see how easily it could happen. To this day I will not take prescription medication for anything.

So between all the attacks on my body from the sickle cell and the side effects of the medication, it was taking a great toll on my body. In fact, my doctor had told my parents that I had sickle cell so bad that they didn't expect me to live to be fourteen years of age; later on they said eighteen. I did not find this out until many years afterward.

CHAPTER 3

A SUNDAY SERVICE

I feel it is only fair to mention that the events that I describe in this chapter have nothing to do specifically with the religion or church that my mother was involved in. This could have happened, and is probably happening, in any religion and in many churches today.

A loving and caring mother took her son to the place where she believed God would meet them, and the healing hand of Jesus would touch him and make him better. When the pastor of the church would give the invitation for those who needed healing to come up, my mother was never hesitant about grabbing my hand and leading (sometimes pulling) me up front for prayer. Many a time the pastor's hand was put on my head and prayers were prayed, and it seemed as nothing happened. This did not stop my mother from having faith that one day a change would take place. This was the extent of my relationship with church and God.

Being about thirteen to fourteen years old now, I began to notice more of what was going on inside and outside the church house. I noticed how the people responded to the word with copious *amens* when it was preached. And the choir sang and shouted with spirit with praises unto God. I noticed how the people worked together when there was a program or a dinner after church. I noticed how they loved God and the people of God and the house of God. I began to understand, or thought I did, how a people could devote part of their lives to the LORD. I saw how a special effort was made to put on their Sunday best to look good when they went to the house of God. Women had their hair done the day before, to look their best when they went to church services on Sunday. Men would have their shoes shined and their suits pressed and fitting when they went to Sunday service. I noticed the pride that was taken when preparation for Sunday service was coming. It might be to be seen a little by others, but it was done to show God how much they wanted to look good for Him. What else did the African Americans have? Worked hard every week, and made enough to survive and maybe save a little for later. Never really got ahead but always looked ahead for a ray of light, some hope—and the Church was where it was found. "God loves you!" was preached which made us feel good, because we felt like not to many other people did. So it was at Sunday service the exchange was made in an attempt to show God how much He was loved.

I do believe that the Word of God is true when it says, in 2 Peter 3:9, that God is "not willing that any man should perish, but all should come to repentance." And it also says in the Book of Ecclesiastes the third chapter, that there is a time and a season for everything under the sun. The time for one of my seasons was about to change.

But is such a small and a powerful word. It has changed the lives of many, and changed the course of many. "I'd like to go to the store with you, *but* I don't think my father will let me go." "I think she is cute, *but* I don't think she likes me." "I would have made it to the interview on time, *but* the traffic was bad." "Dinner would be ready, *but* the stove is not working." I heard a missionary jokingly say once, "I would be a good missionary, *but* the people are different over here."

I don't blame or fault anyone for my actions. They were my decisions, and I have learned to be responsible for my actions. I said that to say this: I probably could have been saved and had a relationship with the LORD a lot earlier in my life, *but* nobody explained to me what a hypocrite was. Therein was the basis to the beginning of my atheistic life that I had for the next ten years. Going to church and Sunday school and watching different ones praise, sing, and shout in the house of the LORD was one thing, but it was another thing to see what I saw later on in the same day.

There's something to be said about being real. We've heard it said so many times: "Just be real." Be who you say you are. If you say you're a football player, be the best football player you can be. If you say you're a wife, be the best wife you can be! And if you say that you are a saint, a Christian, or someone who loves God—well, be that to the best of your ability. It is so important to be who you say you are because others are watching you who want to be football players, wives, or Christians, and they are using your life as the model to go by. I've been told that good advice with a bad example is the recipe for confusion.

CHAPTER 4

A CONFUSED YOUNG MAN

I lived in South Bend, Indiana. I believe the county (St Joseph) if not the whole state was dry on Sundays. That means you are not allowed by law to sell alcoholic beverages of any kind until the following day. Indiana was a dry state; Michigan was not. South Bend was maybe fifteen miles south of Michigan's state line. There was a store on the state line that sold some of the best ice cream that any kid in his right mind would love to have.

Our dad took us up there at times on a Sunday evening after dinner to prove to us that he wasn't all bad, no matter what policies he had in place. While we were there getting ice cream, we also saw some of the very people who'd been in church that morning singing, shouting, and praising God; now they were buying beer and wine! I was confused.

Some might say it was only beer and wine, but to a young person who wanted to believe and who was told that people who went to church didn't smoke, drink, or cuss, this was major. It clashed with all the Sunday school lessons of how God would change you and all the preaching about how, when you get "saved," you don't do the things that you used to do. It was confusing to me. Having an inquisitive mind anyway didn't make the situation any better. Was there a God or not? Did He change people's lives or not? Was this just a game, or just something for people to do on Sundays?

Now the quest began. I needed someone to prove to me that there was a God. And if there was a God, then the people who were confusing me really didn't know Him or love Him like they said or professed they did. Until that happened, I was convinced that there was no God.

CHAPTER 5

AN ATHEIST HEART

A-the-ist – noun 1. a person who denies or disbelieves the existence of a supreme being, (God) or beings.

KJV Psalm 14:1: "The fool hath said in his heart, "There is no God."

Several factors led me to an atheistic heart. First, I was fifteen and running around with friends who didn't go to church, didn't want to go, and weren't made to go like I was. Even when I was made to go as a teenager, it wasn't in my heart to do so. It was just out of obedience and fear and respect for my father.

The more I saw of hypocrisy, the more I looked for it to justify in my mind that there was no God. Some would say if I didn't believe in God that would allow me to do whatever I wanted without any constraints. My argument there would be my father had imposed enough constraints to make up for the ones that I didn't obey from God.

The more I argued with those who said they knew God but were not able to prove it to me, the more my heart became hardened toward the idea of a loving God. Arguing was my way of asking questions and seeing if you truly believed what you were saying. There is a big difference between being told what to believe, and believing what you believe because you believe it!

The fact was that no one could explain to me questions like Where did God came from? How big is God? Does God have a mother and father? Why do we look down when we pray, when you say God is up in heaven? If there is a God and He loves me, when my mother prays for me, why am I still in suffering and pain? I know these may seem like simple questions, but to someone who was confused the simple answer of "That's just the way it is" was not enough.

These questions could have been answered or discussed by a pastor or a youth pastor who was truly concerned about my spiritual growth and well-being. Instead, I got answers like "Look at the sky and the trees, and you will see God." I looked and I didn't see God. One older gentleman responded to me rather angrily, "Prove to me that there is not a God!" I couldn't say to him at that time that the burden of proof was not mine. I sincerely had these questions in my heart and wanted answers, because I was hungry for something and didn't know exactly what it was. I was at an age where my mind and heart were very impressionable, and a concerned person with a Bible and some time could have scored a lot of points for the kingdom of God.

There were attempts to expose us (children) to God, but the most I got out of those vacation Bible schools and retreats was the free food and candy and an opportunity to play a lot of games with other children, something to do for the summer. As a teenager and young adult, being in high school around peers where God just wasn't mentioned as much now, didn't help either. A youngster should be encouraged to think for himself, but with no proper direction, that can be very detrimental. High school would have been a good place to start teaching about religion and theology in my opinion. Biology and science classes only helped me to confirm my suspicions. People would say "Who woke you up this morning?" I would respond, "I woke up myself after my body got enough rest and sleep." They asked, "Where do you think the earth and the stars and the moon came from?" I would respond, "That's easy, the big bang theory." The people trying to address my dilemma didn't have the education that it would have taken to explain that those were just theories. I learned later that a theory was just an educated guess! What I needed was evidence of this God people believed in, people who wanted me to do the same.

CHAPTER 6

A DEATHBED EXPERIENCE

Sickle cell and atheism were my two enemies, and they were determined to take me out physically and spiritually. Sometimes they worked separately and at other times they worked together. As I mentioned before, sickle cell had attempted to turn my doctor into a prophet, for he told my mother that I would not live to reach my eighteenth birthday. Well, as you can see, he picked the right profession of medicine instead of prophecy, because the Bible would have labeled him a false prophet, and he would have been put out of business. But as a doctor he is allowed to make mistakes and still have a practice.

When I was twenty-four, it looked like sickle cell was going to get its wish. I had just come home from the hospital from having a crisis and had been there for about two weeks. My brother-in-law and his wife came over for a visit on a Saturday afternoon in the summer of 1975. We drank a couple of beers and went to see a movie.

Here were two problems that I should have known better than to do. With all the medication that was in my body, I should have never tried to drink any alcohol of any kind. Then the second problem was going into a cold movie theater after coming out of the hospital. It usually took my body a week or two to readjust to what I would call a normal life.

I went into a crisis so bad that I had to be rushed to the emergency room because of the pain I was experiencing. I had been used to dealing with pain when it came to having a crisis, but this time it was different. I could usually take a pain pill, try to warm my body up, and get some rest; usually I soon felt a little better. This time nothing was working, and the pain was only getting worse by the minute. When I finally got to the hospital, the pain was so excruciating that not only was I experiencing the lack of oxygen from my red blood cells sickling, but because of the pain I could not take deep breaths; it literally hurt me to breathe. I received an oxygen mask to force oxygen into my lungs and an IV to start adding fluids to my body. These measures were normal for a sickle cell patient coming to the hospital. What happened next had never happened before. A nurse came to me and told me that they were giving me something for pain and proceeded to give me a shot. That was the last thing that I remembered for that day. She had just given me 40 milligrams of Valium.

The next day when I woke up, I was in an intensive care unit. Several tubes led into and out of my body, and I was hooked up to several monitors beeping and clicking. My mom and dad were outside the room, watching like they always did when I was hospitalized, but what I wasn't used to was seeing a lot of my relatives out there with them. My aunts and uncles almost never came to the hospital to see me when I was there, because it was such a normal occurrence, but this time something was different.

The doctor had come as he usually did and looked at the charts and test results that had been taken throughout the night as usual, but this time what he told my mom and dad prompted them to make a call to the rest of the family. What the doctor told them was that he had exhausted medical science and that there was nothing else he could do for me. If I did not come out of this crisis within twenty-four hours, I would probably die. This was why my relatives were here, coming into the room two at a time and asking, "How do you feel?" Little did I know that they were coming to see me one last time before I died!

Twenty-four hours, and I never knew it until later on in my life. I know the question has been asked, "What would you do if you only had twenty-four hours to live?" A variety of answers are given. But what could you do if you didn't know you had only twenty-four hours to live? Now the answers are few.

One of the people to come and see me was my mother-in-law Maude Thompson (one of the few names that I will mention, and you will hear that name again). She was always concerned about me when I was in the hospital and was always praying for me. She told me later that the LORD had showed her that I had died but had come back to life, and this happened twice. I do remember, but could not explain, waking up one time and looking down on my body lying in the bed and wondering why all those tubes and wires were hooked up to me. I could even see people outside my room waiting to come in to see me. What time this happened I'm not sure, but I am sure that it did happen.

Maude Thompson confirmed what I saw. She not only prayed for me but called a preacher that she knew and asked him to come and pray for me, which he gladly did. His name was Alfred Deeds Jr.; I would later call him Pastor Deeds. He came into the room and looked at me as I was lying there in pain, wondering why I was getting so much attention this time while in the hospital. The first words that he spoke to me were "I know that you are an atheist and don't believe in God, *but* I do." He told me that he was on his way out of town for a meeting but was there because Maude had asked him to come. He laid his hands on me and prayed, and I felt absolutely nothing, but he said that he felt something and prayed for me one more time. These were some of the last words that he said to me before he left: "I know you don't believe in God, but if you will just say 'Thank you, Jesus,' I believe that God will heal you." With that he left and went out of town and said he would be back when he returned from his trip.

What did I have to lose? I was already in more pain than I had ever experienced before, nothing the nurses were giving me was helping at all, and Mrs. Thompson was there to encourage me to say, "Thank you, Jesus," and so I did. When those around you are trying to help you, and you don't understand everything that is going on, obedience goes a long way. "Thank you, Jesus, Thank you, Jesus, Thank you, Jesus." Over and over I said it, with my mother-in-law right there praying as I was forcing the words past the pain that was dominating my body. Little by little I began to doze off and fall asleep.

CHAPTER 7

A VISIT FROM GOD

I was unconscious from Sunday afternoon till Monday morning. The next day when I woke up, I was completely out of pain. This time it was not the medicine that knocked me out and made me sleep but something much more powerful! Any sickle cell patient can tell you that when they go into the hospital in a crisis, they are usually in pain for two to three days before it is under control, not just overnight.

I had no joint pain, no muscle pain, no difficulty breathing—nothing. As I awakened, my body felt as if I had been in a fight all night long; I was totally spent. Thirsty and hungry, I devoured anything the nurses put in front of me, and most of that was liquid. I was not in intensive care for much longer, maybe a day or two, before I was moved to the constant care unit of the hospital. The difference between intensive care and constant care in my opinion was that in the ICU they try to keep you alive, and in the CCU they watch you stay alive. I stayed there for two or three days and was moved to a regular room. After a week I was discharged and allowed to go home.

I stepped out of the hospital, took a deep breath, and said, "Another victory for medical science." You see, I was an atheist, and I didn't believe in God, nor did I believe that God had touched me and made me better. I was used to the medicine and time and attention to get me through the crisis process of having sickle cell. You might ask, What about the preacher praying and the miraculous overnight touch that I received? I just obeyed what the preacher said; I didn't believe what the preacher said. I did what I had to do to get out of that situation. Much like the children of Israel: they did what they had to do for God to show up and deliver them, and then they forgot about all He had done and went back to their old ways of doing things. The only difference was that they knew God and I didn't. They at least acknowledged that there was a God; I didn't. I now believe that the faith of others made up for the faith that I didn't have. More, God had a plan that I didn't know about, and most in that room that day would not have believed it, if God had told them Himself.

That didn't matter to some nor did they understand how that I could have just gone through what I had and still not believe in God, not even go to church and try to say thank you to God. Sorry to say, atheism was grounded into my heart. It was my lifestyle; it was what I believed and lived. I wasn't seeking a God that I didn't believe in—for what? I wasn't a bad person. Most of my relatives thought that I was a good young man. I did well in school. I didn't hurt anyone, and if I saw you on the street and you needed help, I would help you. I wasn't perfect, but neither was I just a terrible person. I was just an atheist; I simply didn't believe in God. No one had proven to me that there was a God, a supreme being that was in control of everything and everyone, and if He was, why was He allowing people to do the things that were wrong?

I had been an atheist for about ten years now, and one of the things that turned me to atheism was still all around me, and still no one explained it to me, and that was hypocrisy. Why were people professing one thing and living another? I was getting more of that than I was getting of someone trying to answer the questions that kept me bound up in atheism. I was still arguing with people and still laughing at them when I was invited to go to church with them when I thought that there were much better things to do like stay home and watch a football or a basketball game on TV.

There was a couple who were my friends. I used to hang out with them to party and have fun together until they got saved and left that lifestyle behind. They went to the church of the pastor who came and prayed for me, and they went to him and asked, "We want to see him saved; what can we do"? They told me later that Pastor Deeds simply told them to pray for me, fast for me, and show me love, and this they did. They would invite me over to dinner at times, and even on my lunch hour I was allowed to come by for a quick sandwich. They were careful not to shove religion down my throat but were wise and thoughtful enough to pray over any food that we ate and pray before I departed from their home. If the subject of God came up, they never brought their Bibles out and started quoting scriptures and showing me how much they knew about the scriptures, but rather told me of their own experiences with God, which I could not deny. They showed me their lifestyle, they showed me a life that was different from when we used to party; now they were living for God. I will talk of them more later on in this book; they are the Millers.

As an atheist, the biggest mistake I made one day was while I was sitting over at my mother-in-law's house after a Sunday dinner (man, she could cook). I was arguing with someone about God and how He wasn't real and how they couldn't prove Him to me. I can't even remember who it was, and it doesn't really matter. What I do remember is what my mother-in-law said at that time.

Maude Thompson was not only a great cook but one of the sweetest women that I have ever met. She never told me I should go to church, though she always invited me. She lived and preached what she believed through her lifestyle. She was soft-spoken but firm when she needed to be and stood her ground when running her household for the LORD. She loved her husband and her children. Her husband didn't go to church, but you would have never known it, the way that she loved and took care of him.

She said to me, "Pray this prayer and mean it. Say, 'God, if you are real, prove yourself to me.'" She added, "If there is no God, you have nothing to be worried about, but if there is a God, He will answer your prayer." I was so sure that there was no God, I thought, *I can do that, that's not a problem, and let's see what happens.* So I prayed "God, if you are real, prove yourself to me."

Little did I understand at the time that I was the king on the throne of my life, and I was in a game of chess against a chess master. Little did I know that God had a plan for my life and was ordering my steps before I even knew Him. And now He had me in a place where He would not defeat me—that was not what He was trying to do but rather dethrone me so that He could be the King on my throne. You may not understand the game of chess, but when your opponent has you in a place where you are not able to contest him or run or hide from him anymore, he simply says, "Checkmate," and the game is over. God had got me to a place where He could say "checkmate" when my mother-in-law got me to pray, "God, if you are real, prove yourself to me."

Can I say something about prayer right here? As I grew up and went to church as a child, I heard the deacons and the pastor pray. I saw when they would either kneel down or stand up and pray at the beginning of a service or maybe at the end. But I never heard or saw them give a class on how to pray. I was encouraged to pray when I was a child by my mom and others, but not taught to pray by anyone. I was asked to pray over meals and at an altar when I was invited to church, but I was never told how to pray. Over the years one of the most important lessons that I have learned about prayer is that it is just talking to God. It's not a long string of pronouns and adjectives that are said to impress others around you; it's just talking to God. It's not the length of time you pray that you use to show your spirituality to others around you; it's just talking to God. I was an atheist, and I didn't know how to pray, nor did I want to. But when I spoke the words that my mother-in-law Maude Thompson told me to say, I said them and only them, and when I did, God heard me and came down from heaven to respond to those nine words: "God, if you are real, prove yourself to me." Little did I know that prayer was just talking to God.

I do not remember the time frame that was involved before this next event happened, but it was no more than a week or two. I don't remember the day of the week or the month, but I do remember this: One night as I lay fast asleep, all of a sudden something woke me and I sat up in the middle of my bed. As I sat there, without any noise, without any rumbling, there appeared a medium blue shimmering light that came from above and went right through me and lit my whole body up! I could see it from the reflection in the mirror that was on the dresser across the room. It lasted for just a few seconds, and then it was gone. It didn't hurt me, and surprisingly it didn't scare me, but it did startle the heck out of me. I wasn't hallucinating because I couldn't do drugs like acid and speed and all of the other drugs that would make you hallucinate; because of sickle cell, I stayed away from all that.

The first question that came to my mind was *Is this God? Is my prayer being answered?* I calmly got out of bed and went into my living room and knelt down. I prayed, "God, is this you, and what is it that I am supposed to do now?" I didn't hear a voice or any response and after a few minutes I got back in bed and went to sleep, but my mind and heart were racing. I am not sure when I got in touch with the Millers, my friends, the next day to tell them of this experience and ask what they thought about it—but that was the next thing that I wanted to do.

CHAPTER 8

A BROKEN HEART
AND A NEW START

You have heard of a crossroads in life or a fork in the road. It usually means a time in your life when you have to make a decision or a major change happens in your life. Well, it was both for me, I was now at a place where I had to make a decision, and that decision would lead to a major change in my life.

I talked to the Millers, and they definitely believed that I'd had a visitation from God and that He was showing me that He did care about me enough to visit me personally. I had to admit that something had happened to me, and the term *atheist* could no longer be used to identify me. I may not have known who He was, but I at least knew *that* He was. I wanted to know for myself who He was, so I had to be real enough with myself to say, *Now what do I do? How do I go forward, what do I say next, and how do I say it?*

Countless thoughts were going through my mind, and this was all new territory to me. Where before my thought process was based upon science and biology and book knowledge and my own logic, now I had to try and process a personal experience and lots of advice from people over time who wanted me to be in church. Because of the time the Millers had put in with me, I was willing to explore a little further.

In the past the Millers not only were nice to me and showed me a lot of love and patience, but they did invite me to go to church with them to experience what they were experiencing. I wasn't the churchgoing type, but in an effort to pay them back for all the love they were showing me, I tried to show them that I wasn't such a bad person, and I could do nice things also. So as my way of paying them back, I would go to church with them. The services didn't have any meaning to me, for I was not searching for any. The members were very nice and friendly and treated me with respect.

Another thing that I want mention at this place is that Sister Miller and her family were very blessed and talented in music and singing. They were very much anointed and used of God with their talents in ministry to bring people to the LORD. That was a very enjoyable part of my visit. I couldn't explain it then, but now I know it was the anointing of the LORD that was (and still is) upon them when they would sing. There is something about the anointing, and when someone preaches, teaches, or sings under it, it will make you listen. It is as if God is speaking or ministering through that person. You do not have to be spiritual to tell whether a person is anointed or not; you will feel it. What you feel is a transfer of what the anointed person is feeling from God to you.

The Hubbards (Sis Miller's maiden name) were very good at singing under the anointing. I would let her know how much I enjoyed her, and she would start letting me know when she would be singing just to invite me to another service. I would go to hear a song and be entertained, but there was always a preached word after the song. Little did I know that as the Word of God went forth it was breaking up the hardened heart of atheism. When the Word was preached, even though I wasn't paying attention to Bible characters that I knew nothing about, the Word of God was breaking up the fallow ground in my life—the stones of unbelief, the rocks of doubt, and the boulders of selfishness.

The Millers were always careful to ask me if I wanted to go up and pray when an altar call was given, which I would usually decline. Trying to be nice, one time I even went to the altar with them to pray, but being an atheist for ten years, I didn't know how to pray and wouldn't. I would just stand there, feeling out of place. Different ones at the altar were excited that I was there and even tried to encourage me to pray. I was doing all this only to show my friends that I appreciated the love they were showing me, and at the same time they were probably thinking that their prayers were being answered.

Time is such a valuable commodity. When used correctly, it will make the difference between heaven and hell. The Millers didn't give up on me after I declined their first invitation to church. They didn't stop showing me love after I didn't accept the gospel that they extended to me the first time. They didn't get frustrated with me (well, maybe they did a little) when I'd walk away time and time again after their attempts to bring me to the

LORD. But they gave me more time in the form of patience. In time a boulder can be reduced to a pebble with just wind and sand. In time a small seed can grow to be a giant redwood. And in time the Word of God can change an atheist's heart to a heart of repentance. At length I found myself wanting to go to church, and not just for the music, but for the Word. Now I found myself trying to read the Bible and asking God to help me understand what I was reading. Time was making a difference.

One Sunday morning, after my visitation from God, I found myself in another service, but this time when the altar call was given no one had to ask me to come up and pray. I had been to enough services to see how others would go up to pray for salvation or forgiveness according to the Word that was preached. I had witnessed the lifestyle of the Millers and others that were professing salvation and the joy of the LORD that they had in their lives. God's Word had worked enough on my heart and life, I'd seen enough, I'd heard enough, and now I believed enough to make a decision to change my life.

When the altar call or invitation was given to come up and accept Christ in my life, I didn't hesitate. I stepped out of the pew where I was standing and went to the altar. There I just turned around and faced the congregation, because that was what I thought I had to do to "join" the church. The pastor—the same pastor who came to my hospital bed and prayed for me when the doctors had given up on me, Pastor Alfred Deeds—instructed me to turn around, kneel at the altar, and ask God to forgive me of my sins.

Something was different this time when I bent my knees and began to pray. Instantly I felt the same as on the night when I had a visitation from God. A brokenness came upon me, and I began to cry to God, not weeping or murmuring but crying my eyes out asking for forgiveness from God. Tears, mucus, and saliva were all mixing together and sliding down my face, but it did not matter to me, because of the cleansing that I felt my soul was getting. Others gathered around me and were praying with me and for the LORD to hear my prayers.

It was strange that I was able to open up and cry so easily, because some four months earlier my father had died, and at his funeral I didn't cry. I just wasn't the crying type, or so I thought. This day was different, God and I were having a conversation, and He was all up in my Kool-Aid, and He was mixing up my favorite flavor, red! I cried and repented and asked God to forgive me of every sin that I had ever done and to save me.

After about ten minutes of heavy praying and crying one of the brothers there at the altar with me said, "Man, you have repented. Now it's time to get you baptized." So I agreed, and Bro Miller took me to a room so that I could change my clothes and prepare to be baptized. I was still praying and crying and thanking God for what He was doing for me. Finally after getting dressed for baptism Bro Miller led our way to the baptismal pool where the pastor was in the water and waiting to baptize me. Before he lowered me into the water, he instructed me when I come up just lift my hands in the air and give God the praise for what He was doing and say, "Thank you, Jesus." Then he baptized me in the Name of Jesus.

When I came up out of the water, I threw up my hands and began to say, "Thank you, Jesus," but instead of English coming out of my mouth, I began to speak a different language. As on the day of Pentecost in Acts 2:4 I was being filled with the Holy Ghost and speaking in tongues as the Spirit was giving me the utterance. I felt like I was given another chance at life, and I was born again of water and of the Spirit. From an atheistic heart to a broken heart for a new start, my life was beginning all over again.

CHAPTER 9

A HUNGRY AND THIRSTY MAN

I can remember us having one of those big family Bibles sitting on the coffee table in the living room when I was a little boy. Every now and then I would attempt to read it and try to understand it, but I got confused and would put it back down. It just didn't make sense to me, and I didn't have anyone at home I could ask about it, because they didn't understand it either. It was a nice piece of decoration for our home. Little did I know that one day God would have me explaining the passages of this holy Book to others who were confused. But first I must be fed!

Being the fourth child of thirteen, I witnessed the majority of my brothers and sister when they came home from the hospital how they had a very healthy appetite and would have to be fed on a constant basis, day and night. I was now that hungry baby, and like the Book of 1 Peter 2:2 says, I was desiring the sincere milk of the Word, that I might grow thereby. God put me on a diet of Word, prayer, and fasting.

Pastor Deeds was an anointed preacher, and we had services four times a week. Tuesday and Thursday was Bible study night, and church service was twice on Sunday. Every now and then Pastor Deeds would have all of the brothers of the Church take a weekend shut-in of prayer and fasting and reading the Word of God. We were challenged to read the New Testament through in one month and start over again the following month. By today's standards this was too much for some people, but for me it was not enough! I wanted more, I longed for more, I desired more; something in my spirit was just not satisfied.

One of the best brothers that God could have joined me up with was one of Sister Miller's brothers, Jerry Hubbard. He ended up living around the corner and down the street from me, which made it convenient for him to take me under his wing and encourage me, praying with me and for me. We studied the scriptures every chance we got and were always looking for another service to go to during the week or weekend.

The Millers were still close to my side, always praying for me and teaching me the Word, and it still was not enough; I was still hungry. So on my own, as I read the Word of God, I would ask in prayer, "LORD, what does this scripture mean?" The LORD might not answer me right then, but always He would give me an answer, either in prayer or maybe in a song or a message that was being preached.

I was one of those who took the pastor's challenge to read through the New Testament once a month. I actually read it through twice during a couple months of that year. Eventually I began to add the Old Testament to that reading cycle, and what started out as a challenge in the long run became God filling up the scripture library in my mind. I used to be pretty good with quoting scriptures by chapter and verse; now what I can't recall, the Holy Ghost will bring to my remembrance.

As I began to add the Old Testament to my reading schedule, the tabernacle in the wilderness began to catch my eye, and my interest grew. I studied more and more on the tabernacle, the Feasts of the High Holy Days of Israel, the Law, and the lives of the nation of Israel. The more I read the Bible, the more questions I had that made me to study that much more. I went to the library and checked out books to get more information on what I was reading, but I would always let the Word of God be my final authority, even if I didn't yet understand it. In time God would always send me the answer one way or another.

There were always radio stations that had preachers and teachers expounding on the Word. One particular program which I listened to on a regular basis was going off the air, and the speaker invited people to come by his church and meet him for one last time. Jerry and I went there and met the pastor who taught on this program.

To this day I cannot tell you what was the name of the church or the name of the pastor, but I do remember while we were there the pastor asked me, "What kind of Bible do you study from?" I told him King James, and he responded by saying, "Yeah, but what kind of

King James Bible?" I showed him the Bible that I had, which was probably given to me when I graduated from high school. I had never read it until now, after I had been born again. He took us into a small library in a storage closet that had a wall full of new Bibles. He reached up and got one and handed to me, and told me that a lady who had been a member of his church had died and left a fund for him to buy and give away so many Bibles a year. That day he gave me a brand-new Scofield Study Bible, and my Bible studying habits changed.

This Bible had so much more than the Bible that I was used to reading and studying from, now I had cross referencing, footnotes, previews of the books, a Hebrew, Greek concordance with lexicon. I was like a kid in a candy shop, but it was all good for my spiritual man. I lived in that Bible and would actually lay it on the bed at night next to my pillow. I studied and studied and studied. If I spent two hours in the Bible before, now I would spend three and four hours. The Word of God was so precious to me, I would ask God to let me walk in the Word and His Word to walk in me. I carried a New Testament pocket Bible in my shirt pocket at all times, so that if I was in line waiting for a cashier, I would just reach in my pocket and start reading. Little did I know God was preparing me for something that would be another chapter in my life.

CHAPTER 10

A CALL TO MINISTRY

A portion of Luke 12:48 states, "For unto whomsoever much is given, of him shall be much required." Six months to a year later I didn't feel worthy to do anything in the church, because I didn't feel I knew enough or had been there long enough to be trusted with anything. I was feeling inferior to those around me, who had been saved longer than I had, and I just never thought that I was good enough. I still felt like a babe in the LORD.

But one Saturday afternoon as I was sitting in my dining room probably studying, I felt this warm presence come over me, and I started crying, because I felt the LORD visiting me, to prepare me to do something that I didn't feel worthy to do. When He would manifest His presence around me, I would feel humbled. It was similar to the feeling that I felt the night I had the first visitation from above. This time I asked God, "What is it that You want me to do?" Although I didn't get an answer right then, that was when I told the LORD, "I will go anywhere You want me to go, and say anything You want me to say, and do anything You want me to do!" I felt that it was the least I could do for God because He had saved me from being an atheist.

I asked my pastor about the experience, and he felt that I might have a calling on my life. A calling? Yes, a calling to the ministry. I didn't feel worthy to be a Christian, let alone to become a minister. Pastor Deeds told me that if it was a calling to the ministry, I should pray, fast, read my Bible as much as possible, and testify in service every chance I got. Why he wanted me to testify every chance I got, he said, was so that I would get used to the anointing coming and going when I spoke.

They still had testimony service back in the seventies, where you could get up and tell the church what God had done for you, or how you were blessed of the LORD in a special way. As awkward as it was for me to get up and try to testify in front of people, I did it. And it was as my pastor had said: I began to feel the anointing of God come down over me and allow me to speak with a different authority and power in my voice. When my testimony was over, I would feel the anointing lift away, and my voice and speech would return to normal. This was different than anything I had ever experienced before in my life, and to me it was a humbling experience. Even to this day, before I preach and I feel the anointing come over me, I will begin to cry.

This did not give me the courage to take a pulpit and start preaching, but it did give me enough courage to ask my pastor what I could do to help around the church. He said I could help in the Sunday school department with bringing children to church on the buses that we had for that. Man, I was so happy and excited to be able to do something for the LORD and the church, and I did it with everything within me, to do the best I could. After about six months I wanted to do more, so my pastor allowed me to assist one of the teachers in Sunday school to teach the young adult class (we called them teenagers back then). So now I was allowed to work the bus ministry and work in the classroom with a teacher. And I still wanted to do more, so I asked if I could join the choir that Sis Miller led, and I got another yes! I was not a professional singer or anything; I never even sang in the glee club at school. I just wanted to do more for the LORD to show Him that I was appreciative for what He had done for me. Besides, there were enough good voices in the choir to drown out my inability to carry a tune in a paper bag.

More time had passed, and now I was asked if I wanted to coteach in the Sunday school. I accepted, not because I thought that I was worthy or capable but because I wanted to do anything I could to help when asked. As I began to teach the class the lessons that I was given, all my studying started to kick in. I knew the scriptures, and I knew the settings to help convey the story, concept, and principles of the lessons. It was a fulfilling experience for me to teach and watch others not just receive what I said but understand what I said.

But there was still this yearning inside me to do more. Something (that's what we call God at times, *something*) inside of me was driving me to do more. I didn't understand why, but I always tried to make myself available to the voice and obey. After I asked the pastor if there was any other way I could help out, he suggested

I help out the ushering department at the church, and I did.

Then during one service, while the announcements were being made, the pastor mentioned that help was needed in the nursing home ministry, and of course I volunteered. The nursing home ministry consisted of four or five of us from the church going to a nursing home in the community on Sunday, where we went from room to room inviting the residents to the dining room or an area where fifteen to twenty could meet. We would pray and sing two or three songs that the elderly residents knew and loved to sing, like "In the Garden" and "The Old Rugged Cross." A minister would preach or teach a ten or fifteen-minute message, after which we would greet and pray individually for all who came to the service.

After I had gone with the team for about three months, one Sunday the leader of the team asked me to minister the Word for that day, and with the grace of God I did. When I finished, I felt like I had preached to a congregation of hundreds. All kind of emotions were flowing for that ten-minute message—fear, joy, pride, and many more. I had just preached my first message, and it felt good. I had a scripture, a thought, and, most important, the anointing. All the times of testifying had paid off. I was comfortable with the anointing, and the word came without effort. All I could say was "Thank you, Jesus!"

Twice a month we did the nursing home ministry, and after six to nine months the leader of the ministry turned it over to me. I faithfully would go and looked forward to going to the residents' rooms and greeting them and asking if they wanted prayer. I looked forward to bringing them out to the dining room and having a church service. It was hard work, but I looked forward to it even if I had to do it by myself at times, because I felt God was using me, even though I didn't feel worthy.

It was in the nursing home that I cut my teeth in learning how to preach a message and begin to use the ministry that God had given me.

CHAPTER 11

A CALL TO THE FOREIGN MISSION FIELD

I spent a total of about five years in Buchanan, Michigan, where Pastor Deeds was the pastor of a church called Bethel Apostolic Tabernacle. Besides the nursing home ministry, I was allowed to preach every now and then at a youth service for a couple of minutes along with other young preachers trying their wings out in the Word of God. Going to the different services and getting to be known by the pastors of those services allowed me to be invited up to testify or speak a few words to the congregation. This would allow me to continue to be familiar with the anointing of the Holy Ghost when it came upon me and use the Word that I continued to study fervently.

I believe the first sermon that I got a chance to preach was at my home church on a Sunday night service. My mother came and watched me stand behind the pulpit and speak under the anointing of the Holy Ghost a simple message that God had given me. I don't remember what the message was, but I know that she was very proud of me, and I was relieved that it was over. My father was not there because he had passed away six months before I got saved. I believe he would have been there if he were alive. My mother-in-law, Maude Thompson, was there and has always been supportive of me and my ministry. As I look back, I can see how God was preparing me for something more than I could ever imagine or dream would ever happen to me.

It is strange how when you are going through a change in your life, you don't see it as a change, but as a trial or a testing of your faith. When it is over, you can see how you came through the fire and were made a better person and are now prepared to go to the next level or phase of your life. I had worked for the city of South Bend for eleven years in the water and wastewater testing laboratory. I started out working for them when I was in high school in my junior and senior years as an after-school job. When I graduated, my plan was to go the Air Force and make a career of it. I had taken all my pretests and had gone to Indianapolis for my physical and swearing-in before leaving for Lackland Air Force Base in San Antonio, Texas. It all went well until I had to sit with a doctor at the end of the physical and the doctor asked if I had any medical problems that they should know about. That was when I told him that I had sickle cell. He began to shake his head and said I couldn't join the Air Force because of it. The news hit me like a blow to my gut, and it just killed my spirit and any plans I had for the future.

When my dad came to pick me up from Indianapolis, he could see how hurt I was and how dejected I felt. He tried to encourage me and said something else would work out for me and not to worry. Well, he was right; something did work out for me because my part-time job in the water testing lab for the City of South Bend turned into a full-time position when I got back. The lab manager said that my good work showed and that I would be an asset to the lab, and they would love to have me work there for as long as I liked. For eleven years I worked in the lab and had worked my way up from a Lab Tech I to a Lab Tech IV in the years while there. I studied and took state certification tests and earned my class B certification, which was, in my opinion and others, a great accomplishment for me.

Everything was going fine until the eagle started pulling the down and feathers out of the nest and start letting the thorns and sticks come through, and was leaving me so little room to rest. I had gotten too comfortable, although I was still doing everything I could find to do with my hands. God was ready for me to leave the nest and start learning how to fly. I thought that the job was playing out because I didn't have a college degree and the younger new employees did. All I could see was that even though I trained a lot of the new people, it was the new people who were taking my position, and as they were being promoted I was being demoted for no reason at all. It was getting uncomfortable in the nest. On top of that, my personal life was going through some major changes that only drew me closer to the LORD. If not for my friend and brother in the LORD, Jerry Hubbard, I am not sure that I would have made it. He kept me lifted up in the LORD, and encouraged me, and let me know that the LORD would get me through this tough, dark time in my life. And He did!

In 1981 God decided to take my ministry to the next level and use me in a different way. I ended up in a church in Baytown, Texas, called Peace Tabernacle, pastored by Lonnie Marcus. Under Pastor Marcus's ministry I learned more dedication and servant hood. Again I worked in the Sunday school department of the church and in any other department where I could lend a hand to help out. I was blessed to be able to come down and get a job at the Baytown Area Water Authority, which was the same type of job but was cleaner and paid twice as much. In about a year and an half I went from plant operator to lab tech and got my Texas certification in about two years. Once again I was starting to get comfortable and settled in where I thought God wanted me.

Then one Sunday evening before church, as the custom was, some came out to the fellowship hall at the church to pray before the service. I was praying, and there were others in the room praying also, when I heard, "Go." At first I thought one of the saints had said it. I turned around to see who it was and whether they were talking to me. I didn't see anyone close enough to me, and everyone was still praying. So I started to pray again, when again I heard it: "Go." Well, I had been saved long enough to have heard and read the story of how God had called young Samuel into service. I believed it was the LORD, and I responded, "Where?" and He said, "Tanzania." Now I wasn't the smartest person in geography and nor was I the dumbest, but for the life of me I didn't know where Tanzania was. I had an idea that it was in Africa, but again I didn't know where in Africa. I remembered the pledge that I had made to the LORD after I got saved: I would go where He wanted me to go, and say what He wanted me to say, and do what He wanted me to do. So I said to the LORD, "If You will open the doors for me to go, I'll go."

I went to my pastor and told him what had just happened. I said, "I believe the LORD wants me to go to Tanzania."

Pastor Marcus said these words to me, which I will always remember: "If it is of God, it will come to pass." It was about the end of summer when that happened, and in November a missionary named Sister Sparks visited our church service. Guess where she was from? That's right, Tanzania. You should've seen my heart jump when

I walked into the sanctuary that night for Wednesday night service and Sis Sparks' banner on the altar that said TANZANIA.

In the church organization that I was in, they would allow their foreign missionaries to come home every four years, visit the churches in the States to show and talk about the work that they were doing in-country and also to raise donations so that they could go back for another four years. Sis Sparks had brought with her pictures and items from Tanzania to show what it was like there, I couldn't look at it enough.

After service I went up and spoke with Sis Sparks and told her about what I thought the LORD wanted me to do. She told me that the head missionary for Tanzania, Brother Simeneaux, was here in Houston, Texas (thirty minutes away), enrolling his son in Bible college. They did need help in Tanzania, and she would give me a number where he could be reached. With my pastor's approval I gave him a call and brought him up to date about what I felt was my call to Tanzania. He gave me information to get in touch with the missionary department of our organization to get the process going.

Now only one more thing was needed to get me to Tanzania: some money! The amount that he said that I would need for supplies and round trip airfare was staggering, and it was more than I had in my piggy bank. I reminded the LORD that if He would open the doors and make a way for me to go, I would go. Now it was getting real. How was I going to get that type of money? My church was excited for me but didn't have the funds. My family and relatives were glad that God wanted to use me in such a way, but they could not provision me to go. So I asked the LORD, "How is this to be done?"

He said, "Start calling pastors in the area and let them know that you have a call to go to a foreign mission field. Ask if you could come for one service to preach, so the congregation might take up an offering to help you go."

Still feeling quite young in the LORD, I just believed God when He spoke to me, and I did just what He said. I started calling brothers I had gone to church with who were now pastoring themselves, and they in return would call other pastors that they knew and thought could help me out. This was beginning to be a lesson in grace and favor, God was beginning to work out things for me to make it all happen. Texas is a big state, but on my job they allowed me to have Sunday and Monday off so that on Saturday, after I got off work, I could travel to the churches where I was preaching. I would preach on Sunday usually two services and then drive back on Monday to be ready to go back to work on Tuesday.

God kept opening doors, and I kept going. Pastors were turning their pulpits over to me, and I would try to preach something that I thought would help them, until the LORD gave me a message that would help them and me. When I preached, the church would usually take up an offering before the message, for which I was very thankful, but after the LORD had given me that one message, after I preached the pastor would take up a second offering that would be twice as much as the first. I preached that message at every church, and God blessed the same way every time. This helped me raise the funds that I needed in half the time I expected. I would be able to buy all the supplies I needed and roundtrip airfare in little more than a year from the time that I heard the LORD say, "Go."

In seventeen hours I went from Houston to Amsterdam to Nairobi, Kenya, then about a three-hour drive from

Nairobi to Moshi, Tanzania. The foreign missions department tried to school me before I went and alerted me to culture shock, which is very real. Brother Simeneaux wanted to wait for two weeks before doing anything to allow for adjusting to the culture, the land, and the people. I was ready in two days!

Bro Simeneaux had allowed God to use him to do a great work in Tanzania in a short amount of time. The government had given him land to develop, and he used it to build a church building and a Bible school with dorms. There was a small studio-sized apartment on the end of the dorms, which was where I stayed. My assignments while there were to help build up the congregation size in Sunday school and Sunday night service and to reach out to the more educated populace such as doctors, nurses, accountants, and such. These were easy assignments because Bro Simeneaux was white, and since I was the first black man that the Tanzanians had seen from America, all doors were opening wide and God gave me grace to walk into the places I needed to be to do His work. I was able to teach Bible studies in the different neighborhood at the homes of the saints who were already in the church when I arrived. I had interpreters for the big classes on Sundays but needed none for the small neighborhood groups because about a third of the Tanzanians could speak fluent English. I was allowed to teach Bible study at the technical school, which was equivalent to our high schools.

God was blessing, and I took advantage of every door that He opened. I had opportunities to meet members of different tribes, and one which stood out was the Masai tribe. The men had long braided hair and wore mostly red, while the women's heads were shaved and they wore mostly blue. They were cattle herders and fierce warriors; most people got out of their way when they came to town because they always had a spear or sword with them, and they were not afraid to use it if they thought that they were being threatened or in trouble. No one that I had met there in my short stay thought it was a good idea to befriend one of the Masai for fear of their life.

While in town one day with the pastor of the church (not the missionary, his job was to build, reach, teach, and send out converts after they were discipled, to reach their own), I saw a Masai warrior near a store. I thought it would be a good idea to take his picture, but the pastor told me that might get me killed, so I asked the pastor if he would interpret for me and he agreed. I asked him to give the Masai my name, tell him that I was from America, and ask for his name. He said his name was Samuel, and it was nice to meet me. I told him to say that where I was from that the people would love to see someone as interesting as him, and would it be okay if I could take a picture with him? Not only did he agree to take a picture with me, but he also agreed to go back to the church compound with me to take some pictures there. Before I left, a Masai had accepted the LORD Jesus as his savior and was baptized in Jesus' Name. I am not sure if he had received the gift of the Holy Ghost, evidenced by speaking in tongues, but I was convinced that the way he worshiped he was filled with something from God.

At one service, a young lady who could only speak Swahili, the language of the Tanzanians, came up to receive the Holy Ghost. When I laid hands on her, she began to speak in English, and I heard her say, "I love you, LORD. I thank you, LORD. I praise you, LORD," over and over again. I believe God did that for me!

While I was there, a well-to-do family had come from Nairobi to visit some relatives and visit the church. They had a five or six-year-old son who had a problem with one of his feet so bad that his mother had to carry him like you would a little baby. They asked me to pray for the little boy; I did and believed God for a miracle. They left, and I never saw them again. That same day I left the compound to go town for something, but when I got back I was told that the father (who was not a believer) of the little boy was looking for me. At first I thought, *What have I done wrong, and why would he be looking for me?* I came to find out that after I prayed for the little boy, his foot swelled up to about twice its normal size. They took him to the doctor, and because the foot had swollen, the skin at the bottom of the foot had become transparent. The doctor saw a worm or a parasite in the bottom of his foot that was causing the problem. The doctor made a cut on the bottom of the foot and removed the worm or parasite, and the swelling went down. The father was looking for me to thank me for praying for his son. This one of many experiences that I had in Tanzania that I will never forget.

After six months it was time to go, I was only supposed to have been there for three months, and God allowed me to stay for a total of six months. I had made many friends and reached doctors, nurses, and an accountant and his fiancée who all got saved. As I left, the Sunday school had grown from about ten to fifty, and the Sunday night service had grown from five to about twenty. God had truly blessed. This was more than I would have ever imagined God would do with me, and I was very thankful for it, but little did I know that God was not through with me yet.

CHAPTER 12

A CALL TO EVANGELISM

I came back from Tanzania a different man. Before I went, I was more shy and timid in my ministry. Now my ministry was more bold and confident because God had shown me what He could do with me when I said yes.

One of the last things Bro Simeneaux told me before I got onto the plane to come home was, "You can do anything that you set your mind to do." He was right, and God had just proven it. After God had said to go to Tanzania, I made my mind up to do everything I could to go. I was more thankful for what I had and how God supplied for me no matter where I was spiritually or geographically. While in Tanzania I met people who lived in mud huts with dirt floors, as well as others houses that are much better than most have over here, but they were all happy with what they had and were willing to give me their best and welcome me into their home. God had opened my eyes and showed me how really blessed we are here in America.

It was good to get back to the States and see family and friends and especially my church brothers and sisters. It was November, the beginning of the holiday season, which made it better, because everybody wanted me to come over and share in their holiday meals while I shared my experiences from Tanzania. I brought back pictures, gifts, and souvenirs just in time for the holiday season as presents for loved ones.

The opportunity opened for me to visit some the area grade schools to share my experiences of Tanzania with some of the children. This I enjoyed very much, because every time I told of my experiences, the eyes of the children just lit up, and their imaginations began to paint the picture of Tanzania from the words that I gave them and the souvenirs that I brought to display.

Soon the holiday season passed, and people were going back to their jobs and normal lives again. I was being asked by just about every one that I knew the same question: "What are you going to do now?" And my answer was the same "I don't know, whatever God tells me." I began to pray about it, and I just didn't feel God wanted me to stay in Baytown anymore; there was something else He wanted me to do. Although my previous job had left a door open for me if I wanted to come back, I didn't feel that was what God wanted me to do.

In 1987 I began to call on some of the pastors who had shared their pulpits so I could get to Tanzania, and they were more than glad to have me come back and preach. Some even wanted me to conduct a weekend of services. As I began to hold services at one church, the pastor would invite fellow pastors to come over and have service with them; in return the visiting pastors would invite me to hold services at their church.

That formed the official start of my evangelism ministry. I had to begin carrying a calendar to keep up with the dates that pastors invited me to preach or hold revivals for them. At first they were just one-night services, mostly on Sunday; then more often I was committed to a weekend of services, like a Friday night, Saturday night, and Sunday morning and night. God was changing my ministry again. I was beginning to preach and teach about winning souls for the kingdom of God. That was a big part of my teaching and upbringing in both the churches that I attended, and now it was what most pastors would bring me in to do, either revive the church congregation and encourage and build them up in the LORD, or renew and restore them to the place of winning souls for the kingdom. A pastor never told me what to preach, but it usually took me just one service to understand or discern what was needed for that church, either uplift or outreach.

Before I went to Tanzania, both churches that I attended held regular revivals with well-known evangelists, and I started noting something that others might keep a record of for themselves. I noticed three things about the evangelists who came by our churches. On the first night, or if it was just one night, each one would have on a black suit with a red tie, and their hair was combed backward. Now this was from 1975 to 1985 before I traveled abroad, so I am not sure if that is still the common practice, and I see many evangelists in the church that I now attend.

When I felt the LORD wanted me to evangelize I asked the LORD for just one thing: please don't let me be like all the other evangelists I have met in my life since being saved. I never owned a black suit or a red tie until I came off the evangelism field, and I just started combing my hair backward about ten years ago. More than just the outward, I didn't want to be the cookie-cutter evangelist. I worked and prayed hard to let the LORD direct me where He wanted me to go for each church where I worked.

I remember being in a service with a prophet at the Baytown church and watched as God would use him to tell us what God had done in his life and the miracles God had used him to do. He later spoke prophecy and healing upon some in the service. After service I went up to him and asked him how I might get that type of power from God. He simply looked at me and said, "You can have it, Bro Hall, if you just pray."

And pray I did, I would always try to make it to service early and ask the pastor if I could just spend some time in his church house alone before service, or if I was there for several days, I would try to set aside part of the daytime to pray in the sanctuary. At one revival I was preaching in central Texas, as I was praying and walking between the pews one morning, God told me to stop at one of the pews at a particular place. He told me that there would be a man sitting at this very place tonight with a heart condition; "If you would call him out for prayer, I will heal him."

Isn't it funny how you think you know more than the LORD at times? I said to the LORD, "But there haven't been very many people coming to this revival, and there is no one that sits in this spot." The LORD simply repeated His message. I said, "Okay, LORD, we will see what happens tonight."

That night in service sitting in the very spot that the LORD had told me were an elderly couple. I mentioned from the pulpit, "Sir, the LORD has shown me that you have a heart problem, is that correct?" He responded and said yes. I said, "If you would come up for prayer, the LORD said He will heal you." He came up, and I prayed and believed God for a healing. Several weeks later I saw his wife at a grocery store and asked how was her husband doing? She said that at a recent checkup, the doctor said he was doing much better. That might not have meant a lot to some people, but to me God was showing me what the prophet had told me: "Just pray"!

As my evangelist ministry began to open up and my date book began to fill up, God told me not to expect to make a lot of money on the evangelism field but rather get ready to be educated. This was going to be a learning experience; God was the teacher, and the church was His classroom. I was blessed to preach in twenty-two different states, hundreds of cities, and hundreds of churches. My eyes were opened to more than most people would see in a lifetime. Most saints know their church and a few others that they may fellowship with, but most never get to see the wide scope of diversity in the body of Christ. There was everything from the far left to the far right with everything in between. And God let me know that they were all His. God showed me how to be all things to all people that I might win all people to Christ.

He showed me how to be abased, and that allowed me to be invited to churches that were in our minds great, with what we would call big-name pastors. On that point let me say God showed me that there are no "BIG *I*'s and little *u*'s" in His kingdom; that concept is only in our mind. He showed me how to be lifted up by keeping Him first and allowing Him to do it, yet at the same time be humble in the midst of people who thought I was great. And all this was not to promote me, but rather Jesus Christ and His kingdom.

God showed me that pastors we hailed as great men of God were really not that great; rather, the pastors we thought were not so great were actually the ones who were always in the face of God. That also goes for the saints: there are people who say or think that they are saved and are not, those whose parents are saved, who are good people and work in the church, but they have never gone to an altar and repented of their sins and been baptized and filled with the Holy Ghost. Some of the worst were the pastors' children, because nobody really could or thought that they should say anything critical of them. If other people could see the problem, surely the pastor and his wife could see it, right?—unless the pastor's wife wasn't being given the attention she needed. It was not unusual for a pastor to put so much time into the church that his wife and children were going by the wayside.

Are you starting to see what God showed me and was teaching me while evangelizing? By this time some are saying, "You are judging, Bro Hall," and I say not I but the Word of God. In fact, God showed me that I can't save or unsave anybody; that's left up to Him and His Word. My assignment was to preach the Word without fear or favor, and by the grace of God I did.

Then there were some saints who thought that they never did enough to be saved. Though they already were, they were very humble and meek and were always at the altar trying to stay right with God. And I do understand that being saved is a process: God forgives us of our sins and washes them away with His precious blood, and we are born again of water and spirit and are saved from our sins. And daily we have to die to the sins and temptations of this world, and we are being saved till He comes for us. Then when God comes and gets us and takes us back to heaven with Him, we will be saved. Hallelujah, Jesus!

God showed what He did, not for me to write a book, but to help the church where I was at the time, to help the pastor with the burden that was upon him and to let him know that God heard his prayers. Then after services were over and the last song was sung and the last prayer was prayed, I packed my stuff, went to the next assignment down the road, and started all over again. And this was without having met the next pastor, sometimes only after talking to him or her on the telephone.

I called a pastor in the state of Georgia one day, and he agreed for me to come by for a Sunday morning and evening service. We had never met except on the phone. Well, when I got there the pastor was shocked to find out that I was a black man. I guess he thought that I sounded white on the phone, and it was okay for me to come to have services with him and his all-white church in the Deep South. Apparently I was the first black man to be allowed in the church, let alone be invited to preach. He didn't know what to do; I was already there, and he had invited me. I could tell he didn't know how his church was going to handle a black person being there and preaching. I was given a warm welcome by the Sunday school superintendent and a big hug and handshake, but that was about all.

Usually pastors would have me come up on the pulpit with them before services would start, but this pastor told me to sit in the congregation until it was time for me to preach. It seemed like all eyes were on my every move, and the pastor was as nervous as a cat on a hot tin roof, not knowing what his congregation was going to do if anything. When it came time for me to preach, I got up and let God use me as I would at any other service. The congregation got behind the preached word and gave their *amen*s of approval.

After the service was over, I thought like most pastors he would invite me over to his house for a meal or take me out to eat and give me a comfortable place to lie down before the night service. That didn't happen. The pastor's wife didn't even come and shake hands with me after service, let alone invite me to their home, I was given a bag of towels just purchased from Walmart to wash up with if I wanted to and showed to a room in the back of the church that had a bed in it that was doubling as a storeroom for things like chalkboards and boxes of items no longer used. The bed was dusty and had not been freshened up in a long time. The pastor gave me a twenty-dollar bill, told me that there was a steak house down the street where I could get something to eat, and said he would see me later for the night service.

By now, some of you are saying that you would not have gone back for the night service, and this I thought about. But then I remembered what God had said, that this was going to be a learning experience. "Okay, God, I get it. Your church has prejudice in it, but I still have to show the love of God to all, no matter what they show me. The body of Christ is not perfect yet; God is still trying to get out every spot, blemish, and wrinkle so He can present a perfect bride to Himself." Some came back that night and wanted to tape the service with their personal recording devices; I said, "This is your church, help yourself." Like I said before, everything from the far left to the far right and everything in between.

I also encountered many good experiences while evangelizing. There were pastors who had evangelist quarters built onto the church for the evangelist to stay, whether for one night or one month. Equipped with a bedroom, bathroom, kitchen, and a living room with a study, they gave a clean and relaxing place to be after a long service. The sanctuary was accessible for prayer during the day. Churches with evangelist quarters would also have the saints take turns and bring by meals on a daily basis, and desserts were plentiful as the sisters and some brothers showed off their culinary skills.

I could share countless stories with you about the evangelist field that God had me on. Many souls came to the LORD, repented of their sins, and were baptized; many were filled with the Holy Ghost. Signs and wonders, healings and deliverances followed the preached Word. I was at some churches for just one service, and the longest stay that I had at any one church was for six weeks, preaching from Wednesday through Sunday and usually twice on Sunday. I traveled from California to Georgia and from Mississippi to Michigan. Pastor Marcus gave me a 1982 Delta 88 with 47,000 miles on it; three years later, before it gave out, it had over 300,000 miles on it.

"Okay, God, You have proven to me that You can open doors for me to preach and minister, and You have definitely given me an education about Your people that no university would ever get close to giving. You have let me see the highs and the lows, the good and the bad, the saved and the unsaved. You have allowed me to see churches that were on fire for You and others that were ice cold and caught up in ritualism. Some would worship You with all their heart, soul, and spirit; some would just go through the motions for You without any heart, soul, or spirit." Then after a while I began to ask, "Why? Why, LORD, are You showing me these things?" I would often remind myself that I was only an atheist saved by grace, but that's not what God saw.

Then one night I had a dream.

CHAPTER 13

A CALL TO PASTOR

The evangelist field was definitely a learning experience, and I learned from all that I experienced. For three years I traveled from church to church, staying in everything from the pastor's home to some of the saints', from elaborate four and five-star hotels to super-economy motels. And wherever a door was opened for me to minister, I was very thankful, and no matter the size of the offering that was taken up, I was thankful. God showed me how to be fully committed, because for the three years that I was on the evangelist field I did not own a house or even rent an apartment; all that I had was in that Delta 88. There were times I was not booked for a week or a weekend when I was given the invitation to come and just stay with some pastors, either in their home or in their evangelist quarters at the church. Family also came in handy when I was in the areas where they lived.

Three years was a long time to travel from church to church, eating everyone else's food but not my own on a daily basis. At times I would ask the pastor's wife what I could do to help out in the kitchen, if I stayed with them; I even volunteered to cook at times.

One pastor in south Texas I preached for several times. He would use a Winnebago that he had parked beside the church for me to stay in. It was nice and convenient, but the pastor told me that every evangelist who stayed in it would end up getting a pastoring job within a short time. That didn't bother me, because I never had a desire to be a pastor. I was just thankful to be saved and thought that I was not worthy to be a pastor, because I was just an atheist saved by grace. That also goes for me being a missionary and an evangelist. The reason I did, was because God asked me, anointed me, and opened the doors for me to do what He asked. I never had a desire to be in the ministry, because I never thought I was good enough.

I don't remember where I was, and I'm not sure it really matters, but one night I had a dream. This is what I saw in the dream: there was this battlefield, and a major battle was going on. I was outside, and it was cold, dark, rainy, and windy, just miserable conditions. I was doing my part on the front lines when a messenger came and got me and said the assistant superintendent of our organization wanted to see me. I was taken to a place so that I could clean up and make myself presentable— from cold, wet, and dirty to being dressed up for a black-tie event. I was taken from the battlefield to a banquet hall that was prepared for a great banquet. When I got there I was honored and given a promotion from the battlefield, for all my time that I had spent there. And then I woke up.

I had no idea what it meant and did not spend a lot of time thinking about it because I had a book of places where I was invited to go and hold revivals. One of those places was a small to medium-size town called Cartersville, Georgia. It was a unique church because the pastor and his wife were white, and the whole congregation was black. When I preached there, what a time we had, singing and shouting, souls being saved, backsliders coming back to the LORD. It was truly a great time in the LORD whenever I preached there.

Before the national conference for that organization the pastor of the church in Cartersville gave me a call and asked if I would come and hold a revival while his wife and he attended the conference. Sure, why not? I enjoyed going there and would always have a great time, and God would be glorified when it was over. In the one week that I was there God saved seven souls, seven backsliders came back to the LORD, and at least seven people were filled with the Holy Ghost. The church was excited, and when the pastor got back the saints ask if I could stay for another week, and the pastor said not at this time. He was the pastor of the church, and I respected his decision.

Later on that year the pastor called again and asked if I could come back for another revival at the end of the year. I agreed, and this time while I was there, the pastor and I had a talk. He explained to me that he was giving up the church and asked me if I wanted to take it over and be the pastor. Wow, I didn't know what to say, but I would pray about it and see what the LORD said. Was this the dream coming to pass? Did the LORD want me to be a pastor now? I didn't know how to pastor, or so I thought. God did tell me that the evangelist field would be a classroom, a learning experience; was this what He was preparing me for? Now it was time for me to fast and pray and seek the LORD's direction on this one.

After a time of prayer, fasting, and consideration, I decided to take the pastor up on the offer. I believe it was on a Wednesday night Bible study that the pastor gave the church the opportunity to ask questions or make comments about his last service before a vote was taken. The pastor asked me to come up and have some words if I would like, and I told the congregation that I loved this church and enjoyed coming to it and ministering, but tonight I would like them to vote the will of God. With that said I went back to my motel room and waited.

A vote was taken and a majority had decided that they wanted me to be their new pastor. I can't say which emotions that hit me were the greatest: joy because they wanted me to be their pastor or some fear because this was an all-new experience for me, something that I had never done before. I guess it was a little the fear of the unknown. Happy, excited, and anxious were some of the other emotions I was feeling at that time.

And I really didn't know where to start! After I was voted in, I can remember standing in front of a people that now trusted me to lead them to this place called heaven, to preach to them and teach them what I knew about the Bible. I stood there not knowing what to say exactly, but these words came to my mind, and this is what I said: "I feel like a couple who just got married, both being virgins, now in their honeymoon suite, looking at each other and saying, 'Now what do we do?'"

The congregation was very kind and receptive, and I would not have known who did not vote for me, because everybody treated me well. I started learning names and positions, I even started little by little to appoint positions and reorganize departments. I brought in ideas and ways that the congregation was not used to but enjoyed the change. I started having meetings with the ministers and even the elders of the church to talk about how and what direction they thought the LORD was taking us.

The word got out that there was a black pastor at the church where there used to be a white pastor, and that brought in the ones that wanted to come before but wouldn't, the visitors, and the curious. The LORD started adding to the church such as should be saved, and the church was growing, and God was blessing! Every service was a new learning experience, and I was trying to take in all that God was trying to teach me. And whether the congregation would admit it or not, God was teaching them also.

I am convinced that God teaches us lessons, and we really don't realize it until we are down the road years later, and we say, "Was that what God was trying to tell me or prepare me for?" To this day I believe that God was still preparing me for the future of things to come, but then little did I know. I wonder if Moses knew that, after he was drawn out of the water and raised in the house of Pharaoh, one day he would be walking through the hot sands of the desert with two to three million stiff-necked rebellious people trying to get them to the Promised Land. He never knew. I wonder if David had any idea that, after watching sheep all day and being called to be anointed king of Israel, the king would try to kill him, and after he finally reached the throne, his own son would run him out of his kingdom. He never knew. For had they known or had we known at the beginning, it would be a different outcome.

As a pastor I did my best to try to encourage, uplift, and teach, do outreach, and influence the community with a positive attitude. I did substitute teaching in the high schools in Cartersville, not for the money but to be a positive influence for the young men in the school. I was by the grace of God able to start a prayer time for the young people who wanted to pray before going to classes every day before school.

As a pastor I was invited to join the Cartersville Ministerial Alliance, which allowed the pastors of Cartersville to join together and help families in need and reach out to the city as a unified body. I noticed that I was the only black church pastor in the alliance, and there were other black pastors in the city. So I reached out several times to bring all the black pastors together so that we could be effective in our communities—to no avail, but I tried.

God led me to start a twenty-four-hour prayer chain for our church, which consisted of one person praying for one hour, then calling the next person on the list to remind them of their hour of commitment, and so on for every hour of the day, seven days a week, week after week. I tried to do anything that God instructed me to do to help the church, the community, and the organization that I was in. I felt I owed Him that much, because He had done so much for me. I could never repay Him, but I was going to do my best and try. There was a prison ministry that God allowed me to get involved with once a week to work in their library with the inmates to check in and check out books. And it seemed I was coming full circle when I was asked to work with the nursing home ministry. I was glad to go and spread the Word and pray with and for the elderly. Whatever I could do to help someone, I tried, because God had done so much for me.

I'd like to think that this would be a good place to end this book, but it's not, because God had more for me.

I gave up the church in Cartersville after three years because I sinned and felt that it was the right thing to do. Yes, I repented, and God forgave me, and my story goes on. I was devastated and I wanted to leave this country and start a new life all over again.

I had called a company that would help me find work in another country. I was going to Australia. I was not going to tell anyone when I left and only would tell my immediate family once I got there and on my feet again, but God would not let me leave. I came back to Texas, and the LORD led me to a church called The City of Refuge in Crosby. There I met the pastor, who is now Dr. Ron Eagleton. If there was ever a time when I needed a place of refuge, it was now. I needed someone who could help restore me to the place where God could use me again to promote the Word of God and the kingdom of God, Pastor Eagleton was the man, and this was the place.

In my first meeting with him, I told him that I was not here to preach but only to help him and the church. I promised him that if I couldn't help him or in any way hurt him or the church, I would leave. We had that conversation over eighteen years ago, and I am still there. He must have not heard me when I told him I was not there to preach, because in a month or so he asked me to preach in a Sunday night service. And when I did, God confirmed to me that He had never left me or taken my calling and anointing from me. Pastor Eagleton has trusted me to oversee the pulpit ministry and allowed me to work with the prison ministry. Another elder, named Anthony Eagleton, and I go every Sunday to teach and preach to a group of inmates in services we call "Iron Sharpening Iron"; what a blessing. I've also written Sunday school curriculum, taught Sunday school, worked with the nursing home ministry, been a cell group leader, and the list goes on by the grace of God.

Its still "What can I do to help?" I still am trying to repay a debt to God for looking down on me one day and in my mind saying, *I know the plans I have for you, and they are not for you to be an atheist, but an ambassador for Me.* Now I am feeling the LORD directing me to the field one more time. This time God wants me to go and give my testimony to as many churches as will allow me to come in and share how He took an atheist and made him an ambassador. Then I will also be able to fill in some of the gaps that I did not have enough pen and paper to tell. I can share some of the other ways God worked miracles for me, and through me glorified His name. It has been an awesome experience, but God is telling me that He has more for me to do. By the grace of God I will do it. I look forward to sharing more of my His-story with you, in Jesus' name.

EPILOGUE

In closing I want to say again: if there is any good or if anyone has been helped by my His-story, I am giving God all the glory. If you have been blessed by this book, please share this book with someone or better yet give them a copy as a gift or just to be a blessing to them.

Thank you for giving me your time, and May God bless you.

CPSIA information can be obtained at www.ICGtesting.com
Printed in the USA
LVOW10s0601101014

408083LV00001B/1/P